To my wonderful Sisters
Kathy & Tricia
Who love, support & inspire me every day!

"Special Thanks to my children (Caroline especially), husband, & friends
for their support & encouragement during this process,
to Penny Weber for her amazing ability to make "Sisters" come alive with her beautiful illustrations!
Also to Janice Onken & Ákos Horváth for their patience & guidance through this new journey for me!"

© 2021 Maryann B. Deignan
Sisters
First edition • 2021

Publisher: IngramSpark
Boston, MA
Website: maryanndeignan.com

Editing: Caroline Deignan
Cover Design & Illustrations: Penny Weber
Interior Formatting: Akos Horvath

ISBN 978-1-7375960-0-4

SISTERS

by Maryann B. Deignan
Illustrated by Penny Weber

Sisters are special friends
put on this earth-
A bond that begins
right at birth.

They share your life experiences right
from the start,
Understanding you from the depths
of their hearts.

Built in best friends who are
second to none,
Play, laugh,
whisper and run.

Doing their best to keep your
worries at bay,
Sisters are the magic that make your
fears go away.

They swoop in when
things get tough,
And put out the fires before
things get rough.

No matter what the situation, your sisters
are there to give you a cuddle,
Pick you up, dust you off, even
when your face may be in a puddle.

There for you as your
mentors and guides,
Sisters inspire you to
reach for the sky.

Navigating life's challenges, childhood,
even those years as a teen,
Sisters are there through it all; the
good, bad and in between.

The lessons learned while growing up
with them by your side…
Watching you grow into the person you
are with great pride.

Of course, there will be times when
you won't see eye-to-eye,
Silly situations that
may make you want to cry.

Senseless fights, disagreements, arguing over toys, clothes, or lies,
Almost always ending in everyone becoming a little more wise.

Loyal, loving,
sweet and giving,
Above all else, it's important for sisters
to be forgiving.

Such trivial things are not worth it and
should always be let go,
So that your bond as sisters
can continue to grow.

Take a moment and listen to your
hearts beat together-
A connection extremely
hard to measure.

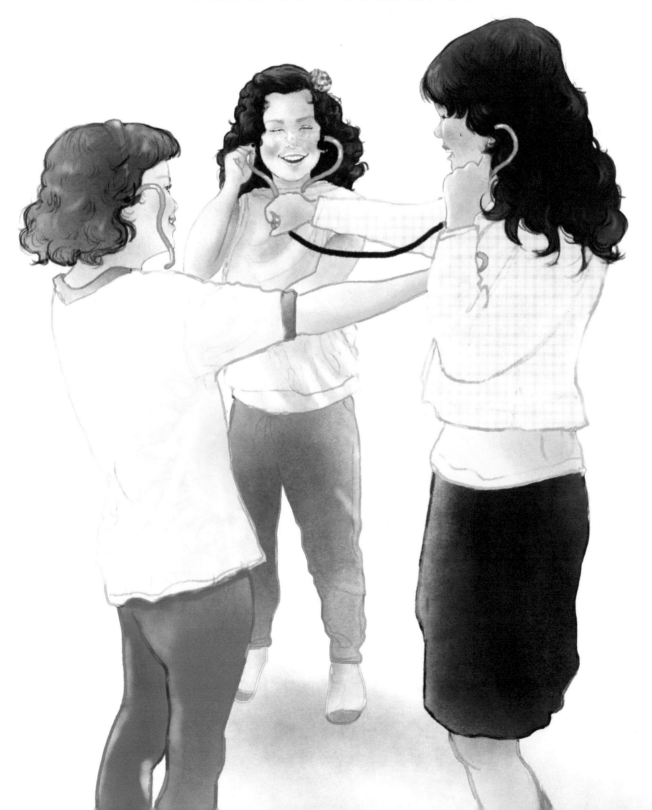

You'll never be alone with
your sisters around,
Even when your world
seems upside down.

So ... always remember to nurture
your sisterly bond,
Today, tomorrow
and beyond.

Penny Weber is a full time illustrator from Long Island, New York.
She works in Photoshop creating digital paintings and has illustrated
many picture books for the trade and educational markets.
Penny lives with her husband, three children
and their fat cat Tiger.

Maryann B. Deignan is the author of Sisters, a children's picture book that brings to light the special bond that sisters can share. Maryann holds a BS in Education and has spent over 43 years as a teacher to children of all ages and abilities. Maryann, along with her husband Chris, opened Kids-A-Lot Country Day School in Stow, Massachusetts. After thirty years as a child care Director, she is now retired and is the proud mother of four grown children. She enjoys spending time with her family and friends on Cape Cod, going to the beach, traveling, reading, walking, crafting, and laughing over a good meal. Maryann resides in Charlestown, MA, with her husband.

*3% of profits of this book will be donated to research & cure of Ovarian Cancer

CPSIA information can be obtained
at www.ICGtesting.com
Printed in the USA
BVHW022317190122
626602BV00007B/414